Let's Move
LIKE THE ANIMALS IN THE FOREST

WRITTEN BY
MARIE-LUISE WEISS

ILLUSTRATED BY
MAURO LIRUSSI

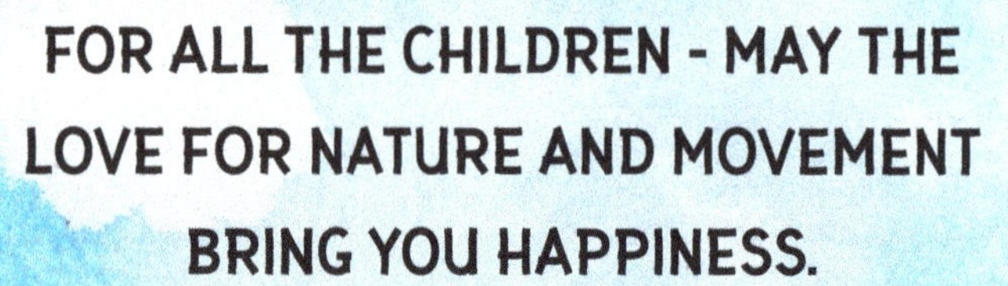

The background information for the educational texts is taken from:
BioKIDS, University of Michigan: http://www.biokids.umich.edu/
U.S. Fish and Wildlife Service: https://www.fws.gov/
National Park Service: https://www.nps.gov/index.htm

Illustrations by Mauro Lirussi
Graphic design by Ara Tatar

Library of Congress Control Number: 2023905865

ISBN 979-8-9880120-0-9 (Hardcover)
ISBN 979-8-9880120-1-6 (Paperback)
ISBN 979-8-9880120-2-3 (eBook)

Published in Piscataway, USA

My dearest friends I welcome you,
And the friendly forest does so too!
Make some room to move and play,
Step inside, you are on your way!

Watch and read,
See and learn,
Now you are ready!
It's your turn!

Walk like a long-legged dainty deer,
Gallop, then stop and prick up your ears.

Tell me, tell me, what do you hear?
There must be something passing near.

Hop like a rabbit, hippity hop!
Paws in the air, let your cottontail bob!

Climb upon the old oak tree,
Being all nutty and squirrely.

Who's that shuffling on four paws?
It's the great big bear – look at his claws!

Now I wonder, do you dare,
To shuffle along like the bear?

Leap like a frog,
Out of your bog.

Then go and hide out,
In your favorite cozy log!

Close your eyes,
You are a mole!
Gently start digging,
Dig your exit hole.

Wiggle (and giggle),
Like a crawly worm.
Coming out of the dark soil,
After the storm.

Spin like a spider,
Spin, spin, spin!
Spin your web,
Until the fly is in!

Roll like a caterpillar,
Curl up tight!
Rock 'n' roll to safety,
Out of sight.

Trot like a fox
Follow the trail.

Keep your balance,
With your bushy tail.

Scurry like a quiet mouse,
Swiftly up into your house.

You come out to play and run,
Only when the day is done.

Swim like a fish,
In the sparkly stream.
Fold your fins,
Catch that sunbeam.

Are you tired?
Well, then rest
Like a hedgehog,
Snuggled in its nest.

Dream a dream,
You are flying high.
Like a birdie,
High up in the sky.

ABOUT THE ANIMALS IN THIS BOOK

• **WHITE-TAILED DEER** walk silently, traveling over open fields and through woodlands. When alarmed, they gallop for escape. The shy but curious creatures can swivel their large ears in the direction of sound, helping them to avoid danger.

White-tailed deer are found from southern Canada to South America.

• **EASTERN COTTONTAILS** spend many hours of the day resting, hidden by shrubs, grasses and woody cover. When happy or excited, they hop into the air doing a "binky," where they twist and kick their feet before landing back on the ground. Eastern cottontails are found in the south of Canada to South America.

• These nut-loving critters have sharp claws which help them climb and descend tree trunks and thin branches. By storing acorns in the ground, and sometimes forgetting about their location, **EURASIAN RED SQUIRRELS** help planting baby oak trees.

Red squirrels are found throughout Europe and Asia.

• Foraging in woodland, **AMERICAN BLACK BEARS** often shuffle flat-footed with all toes on the ground. Sharp claws help them climb trees. They swim for pleasure - and for catching fish.

American black bears are found in Canada, most of the United States into Central Mexico.

• **WOOD FROGS** live in forests far away from ponds but must find water to lay their eggs. When resting, the freeze-tolerant amphibians hide in logs, humus or leaf litter.

Wood frogs live in Canada and the United states.

• **EASTERN MOLES** have large forefeet with webbing in between the toes, which supports digging. The small, velvety and burrowing mammal can dig at high speed. Moles have a fantastic sense of smell! When sniffing, they move their noses back and forth, smelling the source but also where it is located. It is called smelling in stereo.

Eastern Moles are found in northern Mexico, the eastern United States and the southwestern corner of Ontario in Canada.

• **EARTHWORMS** live in damp, moist forest soil. After a rainstorm the segmented crawlers emerge from their moist homes in search of new, even wetter homes! The crawly movement happens when the worm's muscles move, lengthening and shortening the body in wavelike motions.

Earthworms are found worldwide.

• The **MARBLED ORB WEAVER** spins a sticky, silky spiral web. Once the eight-legged arthropod has finished its web, it waits at the far end of the web, in a silken retreat. A signal thread will vibrate when prey gets tangled in the web, letting the spider know of its catch.

Marbled orb weavers are found in Canada and the United States. They are also found across Europe and the northern half of Asia.

• When the **MOTHER OF PEARL MOTH CATERPILLAR** is threatened by a predator like a wasp, it anchors its rear end to the ground, curls up and rolls away at high speed!

The Mother of pearl moth caterpillar is found in Europe.

• The **RED FOX**'s favorite way of traveling through the forest or over open fields is trotting. This way of moving conserves energy. The carnivore has a thick, fluffy and bushy tail which helps balancing and keeps it warm when sleeping in cold weather.

The red fox is found in the northern hemisphere from the Arctic circle to Central America, central Asia, and northern Africa.

• **BROOK TROUT** live in cold, clean and fresh water of streams, creeks or ponds. When actively swimming, the rear half of the fish's body gets most of the work done while the fins are folded back.

Brook trout are native to a wide area of Eastern North America.

• **DEER MICE** are talented jumpers and runners as well as good climbers. The remarkably agile rodents spend their days high up in the hollows of trees or abandoned bird or squirrel nests.

The deer mouse is found in North America.

• **HEDGEHOGS** are mostly active during the night, however some species come out in the daytime. The spiky creatures sleep under bushes, grasses or in tree logs.

Hedgehogs are native to Europe, Asia and Africa.

• **PURPLE FINCHES** forage flying high from tree to tree, looking for seeds, insects, and sometimes berries. Their songs are energetic and bubbly. Male purple finches are raspberry colored, while females have brown coloring with brown and white patterns.

Purple finches are found in the United States, Canada and parts of Mexico.

• With only a single pair of wings, **FLIES** are exceptional fliers! The insects jink, dive and turn to avoid their predators but might still get trapped in a spider's web. Their wings create static electricity, which acts as a magnet for the web, sucking them in!

Flies are found worldwide.

• **WASPS** are often confused for bees; however, bees are hairy, and wasps are not. The flying insects feed mostly on nectar. Their larvae feed on pollen and insects like caterpillars, which mom provides!

Wasps are found around the world, except in the coldest polar regions.

CAN YOU FIND THESE ANIMALS, PLANTS AND FUNGI IN THE FOREST?

ABOUT THE AUTHOR

Marie-Luise Weiss is an Early Childhood Educator and certified Montessori Teacher from New Jersey. Inspired by her passion for music, dance, yoga, and the power of nature, she loves to encourage young children to feel the mood-boosting benefits of physical activity and connect with the natural world. Marie-Luise teaches online classes to children around the globe, as well as music and movement classes to children in daycares and preschools in her area.